GUINEA-B
TRAVEL GUIDE

An African Guide make this Guinea Bissau Travel Guide your companion no you trip

ANDER GODWIN

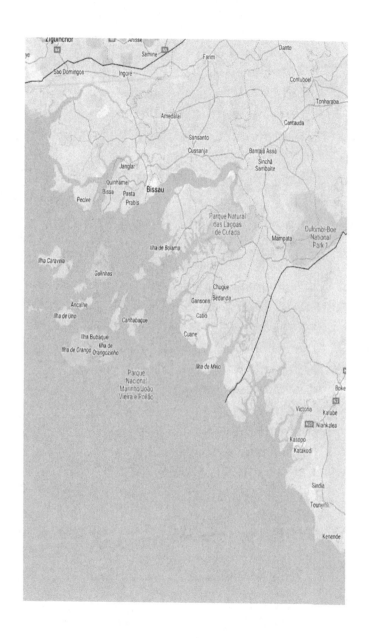

TABLE OF CONTENTS

INTRODUCTION

1.1 Overview of Guinea-Bissau

Welcome to Guinea-Bissau, a captivating and culturally rich country nestled on the West African coast. This section serves as an introduction to the unique tapestry of Guinea-Bissau, offering travelers a glimpse into its history, geography, and cultural diversity.

Historical Background:

Guinea-Bissau, a former Portuguese colony, gained independence in 1973 after a protracted struggle against colonial rule. The country has since navigated a complex political landscape, contributing to its diverse cultural influences and resilient spirit. Visitors will discover remnants of its history through historic sites, monuments, and the enduring warmth of its people.

Cultural Diversity:

Home to a mosaic of ethnic groups, including the Balanta, Fula, Mandinka, and others, Guinea-Bissau celebrates a rich tapestry of traditions. This diversity is reflected in its vibrant music, dance, and festivals. The harmonious coexistence of various ethnicities adds a unique dimension to the cultural experience, creating an atmosphere of acceptance and unity.

Geography and Climate:

Situated on the Atlantic coast, Guinea-Bissau boasts a landscape characterized by mangrove-lined estuaries, tropical forests, and the renowned Bijagos Archipelago. The tropical climate ensures warm temperatures throughout the year, with distinct wet and dry seasons. Travelers can explore diverse ecosystems, from the lush forests of the south to the pristine beaches of the archipelago.

Language and Communication:

Portuguese is the official language of Guinea-Bissau, inherited from its colonial past.

While Portuguese is widely spoken, various local languages, including Creole and native dialects, contribute to the linguistic diversity. A basic understanding of Portuguese phrases can enhance the travel experience, though locals often appreciate efforts to communicate in their native languages.

Contemporary Challenges:

Guinea-Bissau faces challenges, including economic constraints and political instability. However, the resilience and warmth of its people shine through, creating a unique atmosphere that contrasts with its struggles. Travelers are encouraged to approach the country with an open mind, recognizing the strength and determination of the local communities.

As you embark on your journey through Guinea-Bissau, this overview aims to provide a foundation for understanding the country's rich heritage, diverse cultures, and the natural beauty that awaits. Whether exploring historical landmarks, immersing yourself in local traditions, or savoring the flavors of Bissau-Guinean cuisine, your experience in Guinea-Bissau promises to be both enriching and unforgettable.

1.2 Purpose and Scope of the Guinea-Bissau Travel Guide

Welcome to the Guinea-Bissau Travel Guide, your comprehensive companion to exploring the vibrant and culturally rich landscapes of this West African gem. This section outlines the primary objectives and the broad scope of this guide, designed to enhance your travel experience in Guinea-Bissau.

Introduction to Guinea-Bissau:
Gain insight into the historical and cultural tapestry of Guinea-Bissau, offering a foundation for understanding the nuances of this diverse and captivating destination.

Traveler Empowerment:

Empower yourself with essential knowledge and practical tips to plan a successful and enjoyable trip to Guinea-Bissau. Whether you are a first-time visitor or a seasoned traveler, this guide aims to equip you with the information needed for a seamless journey.

Cultural Understanding:
Delve into the heart of Guinea-Bissau's culture, traditions, and local customs. Understand the significance of various festivals, ceremonies, and rituals, fostering a deeper appreciation for the country's rich heritage.

Safety and Well-being:
Prioritize your safety with up-to-date information on potential risks, health considerations, and precautions. This guide aims to provide you with the necessary tools to navigate Guinea-Bissau securely, ensuring a worry-free travel experience.

Optimizing Your Itinerary:

Tailor your itinerary to match your interests and preferences. Whether you are seeking historical landmarks, natural wonders, or cultural experiences, this guide offers insights into the diverse regions and attractions waiting to be explored.

Local Insight:

Benefit from the insider knowledge of a seasoned traveler. The guide goes beyond conventional tourist routes, uncovering hidden gems and off-the-beaten-path destinations to enrich your adventure in Guinea-Bissau.

Cultural Sensitivity:

Foster cultural sensitivity by understanding local etiquette, customs, and traditions. This guide encourages responsible tourism, promoting an immersive experience while respecting the communities and environments you encounter.

Practical Tips and Resources:

Navigate the practicalities of travel, from obtaining necessary visas to managing currency exchanges. This guide provides practical tips on accommodation, transportation, and communication, ensuring you are well-prepared for the journey.

Environmental Consciousness:

Embrace responsible tourism practices and contribute positively to the preservation of Guinea-Bissau's natural beauty. Discover ways to minimize your environmental impact and support local conservation efforts.

Feedback and Continuous Improvement:

Your feedback matters. This guide encourages travelers to share their experiences, suggestions, and insights to contribute to ongoing improvements. The aim is to create a dynamic resource that evolves with the changing landscape of Guinea-Bissau's travel scene.

Embark on your journey with confidence and enthusiasm as you explore Guinea-Bissau's enchanting landscapes, immerse yourself in its vibrant culture, and create lasting memories. This guide is your passport to a remarkable adventure in one of West Africa's hidden treasures.

1.3 Essential Travel Tips for Guinea-Bissau

Embarking on a journey to Guinea-Bissau requires careful planning and consideration. Here are essential travel tips to ensure a smooth and enjoyable experience in this West African gem:

Visa and Entry Requirements:
- Check visa requirements well in advance and ensure your passport is valid for at least six months beyond your planned departure date.
- Verify if you need any additional permits for specific regions or attractions.

Health Precautions:

- Consult a healthcare professional for recommended vaccinations and health precautions, including malaria prophylaxis.
- Carry a basic medical kit with essential medications, and be cautious with food and water consumption to prevent foodborne illnesses.

Currency and Banking:

- The official currency is the West African CFA franc (XOF). Familiarize yourself with the local currency and exchange rates.
- Credit cards may not be widely accepted, so carry sufficient cash. ATMs are available in major cities but may not be reliable in remote areas.

Safety and Security:

- Stay informed about current safety conditions and travel advisories. Check with local authorities or embassy websites for updates.

- Be vigilant in crowded places and keep an eye on personal belongings to prevent theft.

Local Customs and Etiquette:
- Respect local customs and traditions. It's customary to greet people with a handshake and a polite inquiry about their well-being.
- Ask for permission before taking photographs of locals, especially in rural areas.

Language:
- Portuguese is the official language, but various local languages are spoken. Basic Portuguese phrases can be helpful, but English may not be widely understood, particularly in rural areas.

Transportation:
- Arrange transportation in advance, especially for inter-city travel. Public transportation may not be as reliable, so consider private options.
- Road conditions can vary, so plan for longer travel times between destinations.

Accommodation:

- Book accommodations in advance, especially during peak travel seasons. Options range from budget guesthouses to luxury hotels.
- Consider staying in eco-friendly or locally-owned establishments to support sustainable tourism.

Climate and Packing:

- Guinea-Bissau has a tropical climate, so pack lightweight, breathable clothing. Include a light jacket for cooler evenings and rain showers.
- Sunscreen, insect repellent, and a reusable water bottle are essential items.

Cultural Sensitivity:

- Dress modestly, especially in rural areas and religious sites.
- Seek permission before entering someone's home and remove shoes if required.

Time Zone:

- Guinea-Bissau operates on Greenwich Mean Time (GMT). Confirm the local time and adjust your schedule accordingly.

Local Cuisine:
- Embrace the local culinary scene but exercise caution with street food. Choose well-cooked and freshly prepared meals to avoid foodborne illnesses.

Communication:
- Purchase a local SIM card for your phone for easier communication within the country.
- Learn a few basic phrases in Portuguese to enhance your interaction with locals.

Responsible Tourism:
- Respect the environment and local communities. Avoid littering and participate in community-based tourism initiatives when possible.

By adhering to these essential travel tips, you'll not only enhance your safety and well-being but also contribute to a positive and respectful experience in Guinea-Bissau.

UNDERSTANDING GUINEA BISSAU

2.1 Brief History and Cultural Background of Guinea-Bissau

Pre-Colonial Era

Guinea-Bissau, nestled on the West African coast, has a rich history dating back to ancient times. Before the arrival of European colonizers, the region was home to diverse ethnic groups, each with its own unique customs, languages, and social structures. The Bijagos Archipelago, with its prehistoric megaliths, stands testament to the early habitation of the area.

Portuguese Colonization

In the 15th century, Portuguese explorers began their maritime ventures along the West African coast. Guinea-Bissau fell under Portuguese control during the colonial era, becoming an integral part of the transatlantic slave trade. Centuries of colonization left a lasting impact on the country's culture, language, and social dynamics.

Struggle for Independence

The mid-20th century witnessed a surge of nationalist movements across Africa, and Guinea-Bissau was no exception. Led by charismatic leaders like Amílcar Cabral, the African Party for the Independence of Guinea and Cape Verde (PAIGC) fought a protracted war against Portuguese colonial rule. The country finally gained independence on September 24, 1973, with Luis Cabral becoming its first president.

Post-Independence Challenges

Despite the euphoria of independence, Guinea-Bissau faced numerous challenges, including political instability and internal conflicts. The country experienced a series of coups and political upheavals, affecting its socio-economic development.

Contemporary Developments

In recent years, Guinea-Bissau has made efforts to stabilize its political landscape. The restoration of multiparty democracy and international support have contributed to a more positive trajectory. The resilience of its people and their commitment to democratic governance mark a promising phase in the country's contemporary history.

Cultural Background

Ethnic Diversity

Guinea-Bissau boasts a mosaic of ethnic groups, each with its own distinct traditions and languages. The Fulani, Balanta, Mandinka, and Pepel are among the major ethnic communities, contributing to the country's vibrant cultural tapestry.

Languages and Communication

Portuguese serves as the official language, a legacy of colonial rule. However, various ethnic languages, including Creole, Fula, and Balanta, are widely spoken, reflecting the country's linguistic diversity.

Arts and Music

The arts play a significant role in Guinea-Bissau's cultural expression. Traditional music, characterized by rhythmic beats and vibrant dance, reflects the spirit of the people. The country has produced renowned musicians who blend traditional sounds with modern influences.

Festivals and Celebrations

Guinea-Bissau's festivals are colorful and lively, showcasing the cultural richness of its people. The Carnival of Bissau and the traditional Mask Dance Festival are among the celebrations that offer a glimpse into the nation's heritage.

Understanding Guinea-Bissau's history and cultural background provides travelers with a deeper appreciation for the destination, fostering a more meaningful and immersive travel experience.

2.2 Geography and Climate

Guinea-Bissau, a small West African country, is characterized by diverse landscapes and a tropical climate. Understanding the geography and climate is crucial for planning a successful and enjoyable trip.

Geography:

- **Location:** Situated on the Atlantic coast, Guinea-Bissau shares borders with Senegal to the north and Guinea to the south and east. It also encompasses the Bijagos Archipelago.
- **Terrain:** The country features a mix of coastal plains, mangrove swamps, and low-lying hills. The interior includes savannahs and tropical forests.

Climate:

- **Tropical Climate:** Guinea-Bissau experiences a tropical climate with distinct wet and dry seasons.

- **Rainy Season:** The rainy season typically spans from June to October. During this period, heavy rainfall is common, fostering lush green landscapes. Travelers should be prepared for occasional downpours and increased humidity.

- **Dry Season:** From November to May, Guinea-Bissau witnesses the dry season, characterized by lower humidity and less precipitation. This period is ideal for travel and outdoor activities.

- **Temperature:** Temperatures remain relatively consistent throughout the year, ranging from 24°C to 30°C (75°F to 86°F). Coastal areas may experience milder temperatures, while inland regions may be warmer.

Bijagos Archipelago:

- **Unique Ecosystem:** The Bijagos Archipelago, comprising numerous islands, boasts a distinct ecology. Mangroves, sandy beaches, and diverse marine life contribute to its unique charm.

- **Wildlife Sanctuary:** The archipelago is recognized as a UNESCO Biosphere Reserve, home to diverse species, including sea turtles, hippos, and various bird species.

Environmental Considerations:

- **Conservation Efforts:** Guinea-Bissau places importance on environmental conservation. Visitors are encouraged to respect natural habitats, follow eco-friendly practices, and support local initiatives for sustainability.

- **Mangrove Preservation:** The mangrove ecosystems, crucial for biodiversity, are actively conserved. Travelers can explore these areas responsibly to appreciate their ecological significance.

Seasonal Considerations:

- **Festivals and Events:** Travelers may wish to plan their visits around local festivals and events. The timing of festivals can vary, so checking the local calendar is advisable for an enriched cultural experience.

- **Wildlife Spotting:** The dry season is conducive to wildlife spotting, particularly in the Bijagos Archipelago. Sea turtles nesting and diverse bird species make this period favorable for nature enthusiasts.

Understanding Guinea-Bissau's geography and climate provides the foundation for a well-prepared and enjoyable travel experience. Whether exploring the bustling city of Bissau, venturing into the interior, or relaxing on the pristine beaches of the Bijagos Archipelago, being attuned to the country's natural rhythms enhances the overall journey.

2.3 Languages Spoken in Guinea-Bissau

Guinea-Bissau, a culturally diverse and vibrant country, boasts a rich linguistic landscape reflective of its historical and ethnic diversity. The official language of Guinea-Bissau is Portuguese, a legacy of its colonial past. However, this linguistic foundation does not encapsulate the full extent of the country's linguistic diversity. Here is a detailed exploration of the languages spoken in Guinea-Bissau:

Portuguese:

- **Usage:** Portuguese serves as the official language, employed in government, education, and official communications.
- **Local Interaction:** While many urban dwellers are proficient in Portuguese, in more rural areas, local dialects may take precedence in daily communication.

Kriol (Crioulo):

- **Origin and Influence:** Kriol, a Portuguese-based creole, is widely spoken as a lingua franca among the various ethnic groups.
- **Communication:** Commonly used for informal communication, Kriol is an

essential tool for travelers to engage in everyday conversations with locals.

Fula (Pulaar):

- **Distribution:** Fula is predominantly spoken by the Fula ethnic group, particularly in the eastern regions of Guinea-Bissau.
- **Significance:** It plays a crucial role in fostering communication within the Fula community.

Mandinka (Mandinga):

- **Community Usage:** Mandinka is spoken by the Mandinka ethnic group, primarily residing in the northeastern part of the country.iii
- **Cultural Identity:** The language is integral to the preservation of Mandinka culture and traditions.

Balanta:

- **Ethnic Significance:** The Balanta people, one of the largest ethnic groups, use the Balanta language as a means of cultural expression and identity.

- **Cultural Context:** Understanding Balanta can offer insights into the rich cultural tapestry of the country.

Manjaku (Manjak):

- **Regional Usage:** The Manjaku language is prevalent in the northwest, particularly among the Manjaku ethnic group.
- **Cultural Heritage:** Knowledge of Manjaku contributes to a deeper appreciation of the traditions of this ethnic community.

Papel:

- **Community Context:** Papel is spoken by the Papel people, mainly residing in the coastal regions of Guinea-Bissau.
- **Ceremonial Role:** This language is often used in traditional ceremonies and rituals.

Understanding the linguistic diversity of Guinea-Bissau enhances the travel experience by fostering cultural exchange and facilitating communication with the warm and diverse local population. Travelers are encouraged to learn basic

Portuguese phrases and embrace the local languages for a more immersive and rewarding journey through this West African gem.

PREPARATION AND PLANNING

3.1 Travel Requirements and Visa Information

Visa Regulations

1. Entry Visa

Guinea-Bissau welcomes travelers from around the world, and obtaining a visa is a crucial step for most visitors. Visa requirements may vary based on your nationality, so it's essential to check with the nearest Guinea-Bissau embassy or consulate well in advance of your planned trip.

- **Tourist Visa:** Typically required for short-term visits. Ensure you apply for a tourist visa before your departure, allowing for sufficient processing time.
- **Business Visa:** If your visit is for business purposes, a specific business visa might be

necessary. Confirm the requirements and documentation needed for a smooth application process.

Visa Application Process

1. Required Documentation

When applying for a visa to Guinea-Bissau, be prepared to submit the following documents:

- Passport with at least six months' validity beyond your intended departure date.
- Completed visa application form.
- Passport-size photographs meeting specific requirements.
- Proof of travel arrangements, including flight itinerary.
- Hotel reservations or a letter of invitation from a host in Guinea-Bissau.

2. Visa Fees

- Check the current visa fees, which can vary based on the type and duration of the visa.

Fees are often payable in the local currency or an accepted foreign currency.

3. Processing Time

- Start the visa application process well in advance, as processing times can vary. Expedited processing may be available for an additional fee.

Visa on Arrival

Guinea-Bissau offers visa on arrival for certain nationalities, but availability and conditions can change. Confirm the latest information before relying on this option.

Visa Extensions

If you plan to extend your stay beyond the initially approved period, inquire about the possibility of visa extensions. Extensions are subject to local immigration regulations.

Entry and Exit Requirements

1. Yellow Fever Vaccination

A yellow fever vaccination certificate is often mandatory for entry into Guinea-Bissau. Ensure you have this vaccination and carry the certificate with you.

2. Health Insurance

While not always mandatory, having comprehensive health insurance is highly recommended to cover potential medical expenses during your stay.

Border Crossings

Understand the available entry points and border crossing procedures. Some border areas may have specific regulations, so be aware of the requirements for a smooth transit.

Travel Advisories

Before finalizing your travel plans, check for any travel advisories issued by your government. Stay informed about the current situation in Guinea-Bissau to ensure a safe and enjoyable trip.

3.2 Health and Vaccination Recommendations

Overview of Health Conditions

Guinea-Bissau, like many tropical destinations, presents certain health considerations for travelers. Understanding and addressing these concerns is crucial to ensure a safe and enjoyable journey. This section provides a comprehensive overview of health conditions in Guinea-Bissau.

Common Health Risks

a. Malaria: Guinea-Bissau is a malaria-endemic country. Travelers should take antimalarial medication as prescribed by a healthcare professional and use insect repellent, long-sleeved clothing, and bed nets to minimize the risk of mosquito bites.

b. Yellow Fever: A yellow fever vaccination is mandatory for all travelers entering Guinea-Bissau. Ensure you have a valid yellow fever certificate, and consider getting the vaccine well in advance of your trip.

c. **Waterborne Diseases:** Exercise caution with food and water consumption to prevent diseases such as cholera and traveler's diarrhea. Stick to bottled or treated water, avoid consuming raw or undercooked food, and practice good hand hygiene.

Recommended Vaccinations

a. **Routine Vaccinations:** Ensure routine vaccinations, including measles, mumps, rubella (MMR), diphtheria, tetanus, and pertussis (DTP), are up-to-date before traveling to Guinea-Bissau.

b. **Hepatitis A and B:** Vaccination against hepatitis A and B is advisable for all travelers, as these diseases can be transmitted through contaminated food, water, or bodily fluids.

c. **Meningitis:** Depending on the time of year and specific travel plans, vaccination against meningitis may be recommended. Check with your healthcare provider for the latest advice.

Health Precautions and Tips

a. Medical Insurance: Ensure you have comprehensive travel insurance that covers medical expenses, including evacuation if necessary.

b. Medical Facilities: Medical facilities in Guinea-Bissau may be limited, especially in rural areas. Identify the nearest healthcare facilities in advance and carry a basic first-aid kit.

c. Food and Water Safety: Consume only well-cooked food, avoid street food in high-risk areas, and drink bottled or treated water. Peel fruits and vegetables before consumption.

d. Insect Protection: Use insect repellent containing DEET, wear long sleeves and pants, and sleep under a mosquito net, especially in malaria-prone regions.

Traveler's Health Checklist

a. Consult with a healthcare professional for personalized health advice based on your medical history and travel plans.

b. Pack necessary medications, along with a copy of prescriptions, in your travel medical kit.

c. Stay informed about the latest health advisories and updates before and during your trip.

d. Carry a list of emergency contacts, including local healthcare providers and embassy contacts.

By prioritizing your health and taking necessary precautions, you can minimize health risks and fully enjoy your exploration of Guinea-Bissau. Always consult with a healthcare professional well in advance of your journey to ensure you receive the most accurate and up-to-date health recommendations tailored to your individual needs.

3.3 Currency and Money Matters in Guinea-Bissau

Guinea-Bissau, like many West African countries, has its own currency. Understanding the local currency, banking options, and financial practices is crucial for a smooth and enjoyable travel experience. Here's a detailed overview of currency and money matters in Guinea-Bissau:

Currency: West African CFA Franc (XOF)

- Guinea-Bissau uses the West African CFA franc as its official currency. The currency code is XOF, and it is pegged to the Euro. The notes and coins come in denominations of 500, 1,000, 2,000, 5,000, and 10,000 francs.

Currency Exchange:

- Currency exchange services are available at major airports, banks, and exchange bureaus in urban areas like Bissau. It's advisable to exchange some currency upon arrival for immediate expenses.

- US Dollars and Euros are widely accepted for exchange, but it's recommended to carry smaller denominations for convenience.

ATMs and Banking:

- In Bissau and larger cities, you'll find ATMs that accept international credit and debit cards. However, it's important to note that in more remote areas, ATMs may be scarce.
- Banking hours are typically from Monday to Friday, with limited services on Saturdays. Major banks include Banco Central de Guiné-Bissau and Ecobank.

Credit Cards:

- Credit cards are not universally accepted, and it's common for businesses and services to prefer cash transactions. Visa and Mastercard are more widely accepted than other cards.

- It's advisable to inform your bank about your travel plans to avoid any potential issues with card transactions.

Traveler's Checks:

- Traveler's checks are not widely accepted in Guinea-Bissau, and it may be challenging to find places that will cash them. It's recommended to rely on a combination of cash and cards.

Local Spending Tips:

- Bargaining is a common practice in markets, but it may not be as prevalent in established shops.
- Tipping is not mandatory but is appreciated. A small tip for good service is customary in restaurants.

Safety and Security:

- Exercise caution when carrying large sums of money. Use hotel safes or other secure options.
- Be vigilant at ATMs and use machines located in well-lit and populated areas.

Currency Regulations:
- There are no restrictions on the import or export of local or foreign currency. However, it's advisable to declare amounts over a certain limit at customs.

Understanding the currency and money matters in Guinea-Bissau is essential for a hassle-free travel experience. Having a mix of cash, cards, and knowledge of local financial practices ensures that you can navigate the country's financial landscape with confidence.

3.4 Safety and Security Tips

Guinea-Bissau, with its rich cultural tapestry and natural beauty, offers a unique travel experience.

However, like any destination, it is essential to prioritize safety and be aware of potential risks. This chapter provides comprehensive safety and security tips to ensure a secure and enjoyable journey.

Travel Advisories and Pre-Trip Research

- Check for the latest travel advisories and updates from reputable sources such as government travel websites and international organizations.
- Research the current political and social situation in Guinea-Bissau to make informed decisions about your travel plans.

Health and Medical Precautions

- Consult with a healthcare professional well in advance to receive necessary vaccinations and health advice.
- Carry a basic first aid kit and any prescribed medications, as access to specific medicines may be limited.

Personal Safety Measures

- Be cautious of your surroundings, especially in crowded or unfamiliar areas.
- Keep valuables secure and use anti-theft devices such as money belts for important documents and currency.

Local Laws and Customs

- Familiarize yourself with local laws and customs to avoid unintentional legal issues.
- Respect cultural norms, particularly regarding dress code and photography restrictions in certain areas.

Transportation Safety

- Use reputable transportation providers and adhere to safety guidelines when using public or private transportation.
- Be cautious when traveling at night, and consider the condition of roads and vehicles.

Accommodation Security

- Choose accommodations with good security measures, such as well-lit entrances, secure locks, and reputable staff.
- Safeguard your room key and use hotel safes for valuable items.

Communication and Emergency Contacts

- Keep a local SIM card for communication within Guinea-Bissau and ensure your phone is charged.
- Save emergency contacts, including local authorities and the nearest embassy or consulate.

Natural and Environmental Risks

- Be aware of local weather conditions and potential natural risks, such as floods or tropical diseases.
- Follow guidelines for outdoor activities, particularly in remote or natural areas.

Cultural Sensitivity for Personal Safety

- Understand and respect cultural differences to minimize misunderstandings.
- Avoid discussing sensitive topics and be mindful of local customs, especially in rural or traditional communities.

Group Travel and Safety Briefings

- If traveling in a group, establish a communication plan and emergency procedures.
- Conduct safety briefings before engaging in adventurous activities or exploring less-frequented areas.

Insurance Coverage

- Obtain comprehensive travel insurance covering medical emergencies, trip cancellations, and other unforeseen events.

Remember, while Guinea-Bissau is generally welcoming to tourists, staying informed and practicing common-sense safety measures enhances the overall travel experience. Regularly check for updates and stay connected with local authorities for the latest information during your stay.

GETTING THERE AND AROUND

4.1 International Airports and Entry Points

Guinea-Bissau, though relatively compact, offers convenient international entry points, facilitating access for travelers from various parts of the world. The primary gateway to the country is the Osvaldo Vieira International Airport located in the capital city, Bissau. Here's a detailed overview of the international airports and key entry points in Guinea-Bissau:

Osvaldo Vieira International Airport (OXB) - Bissau

- **Location:** Bissau, the capital city of Guinea-Bissau.

- **Facilities:** Osvaldo Vieira International Airport is equipped with essential facilities, including customs, immigration, and baggage services. It serves as a hub connecting Guinea-Bissau to international destinations.

- **Airlines:** Several international airlines operate flights to and from Osvaldo Vieira International Airport, establishing connections to Europe, West Africa, and other parts of the world.

- **Transportation:** The airport is approximately 11 kilometers from the city center. Travelers can access the city by taxi or pre-arranged transportation services.

Bubaque Airport (BQE) - Bijagos Archipelago

- **Location:** Bubaque, serving the Bijagos Archipelago.

- **Access:** Bubaque Airport plays a crucial role in connecting travelers to the stunning Bijagos Archipelago. It primarily handles domestic flights but may also have occasional international charter flights.

- **Island Hopping:** Travelers planning to explore the Bijagos Archipelago often use Bubaque Airport as a starting point for island-hopping adventures.

Other Airports and Airfields

- In addition to Osvaldo Vieira and Bubaque, Guinea-Bissau has several smaller airports and airstrips in various regions. These may cater to domestic flights and occasional charters.

- Notable airfields include those in cities like Bafatá, Bubaque, and Gabú, providing options for regional travel within the country.

Seaports and Water Entry Points

- Given Guinea-Bissau's coastal geography, seaports also serve as significant entry points. Bissau Port, in the capital, is a key maritime gateway for cargo and passenger ships.

- The Bijagos Archipelago has multiple ferry services connecting islands and offering an alternative mode of entry for those seeking a maritime adventure.

Traveler's Tip: It's advisable to check for any travel restrictions, visa requirements, and flight availability before planning your trip. Osvaldo Vieira International Airport remains the primary choice for international travelers, offering seamless access to the diverse landscapes and cultural experiences that Guinea-Bissau has to offer.

As you embark on your journey, the international airports and entry points in Guinea-Bissau are your gateways to a rich and rewarding exploration of this vibrant West African nation.

4.2   Domestic   Transportation Options

Navigating Guinea-Bissau's diverse landscapes and vibrant cities requires a reliable understanding of the available domestic transportation options. From bustling urban centers to remote natural wonders, the country offers several means of travel to suit different preferences and budgets.

Road Transportation:

Guinea-Bissau's road network connects major cities and rural areas, providing an immersive way to experience the country. Travelers can choose from various modes of road transportation:

- **Taxis:** Taxis are prevalent in urban areas, particularly in Bissau. Negotiate fares before starting your journey, and ensure the vehicle is in good condition.
- **Car Rentals:** Rental agencies operate in major cities, offering self-drive options or

chauffeur-driven services. It's advisable to book in advance, and be aware of road conditions, especially in rural areas.

- **Bush Taxis:** Shared minivans, known as bush taxis or "toke-tokes," are a common mode of transport between towns and villages. While cost-effective, they may be less comfortable and adhere to flexible schedules.

Air Transportation:

Guinea-Bissau has a limited but functional domestic air network, connecting major cities and islands. Key points regarding air transportation include:

- **Domestic Flights:** Bissau Osvaldo Vieira International Airport serves as the primary hub for domestic flights. Airlines like TACV Cabo Verde and Ceiba Intercontinental operate routes to cities such as Bafatá and Gabú.

- **Island Hopping:** For those exploring the Bijagos Archipelago, domestic flights or ferry services are available to reach islands like Bubaque and Orango.

Water Transportation:

Given Guinea-Bissau's coastal geography and river systems, water transportation plays a crucial role. Options include:

- **Ferries:** Ferries operate on rivers and coastal areas, connecting cities and facilitating transportation of goods and passengers.
- **Pirogues:** Traditional wooden boats known as pirogues are commonly used for river transport. They offer a unique and scenic way to travel between villages along the many waterways.

Railway Transportation:

Guinea-Bissau currently does not have a comprehensive railway network. Travelers rely primarily on roads and other means of transportation.

Travel Tips:

- **Flexibility:** While domestic transportation options are available, schedules may be subject to change. It's advisable to be flexible with plans, especially when using shared modes of transport.

- **Local Advice:** Consult locals or your accommodation for the most up-to-date information on transportation options, as conditions and services may vary.

- **Traveling Off the Beaten Path:** Exploring remote regions may require a combination of transportation modes. Seek guidance from experienced local guides for such journeys.

Understanding the domestic transportation landscape in Guinea-Bissau enhances the overall travel experience, allowing visitors to navigate the country efficiently and explore its rich cultural and natural diversity.

4.3 Tips for Navigating Local Transportation in Guinea-Bissau

Guinea-Bissau offers a diverse array of local transportation options that cater to both urban and rural settings. Navigating these transportation systems efficiently can greatly enhance your travel experience. Here are some valuable tips to help you get around:

Understanding Transportation Hubs:
Familiarize yourself with key transportation hubs, especially in the capital city, Bissau. The main hub is Osvaldo Vieira International Airport, and the Bissau-Bandim transport interchange is crucial for local buses and taxis.

Public Buses:

Public buses are a common mode of transportation within Bissau and other major towns. While schedules may not always be strictly adhered to, buses offer an affordable way to explore the city. Check with locals or at bus terminals for route information.

Taxis and Shared Taxis:
Taxis are readily available in urban areas, and they are usually unmetered. Agree on the fare before starting your journey. Shared taxis, identifiable by their specific routes, are a cost-effective option for short distances.

Car Rentals:
For more independence and the flexibility to explore remote areas, consider renting a car. Ensure you have the necessary permits and are aware of local driving regulations. Roads may vary in quality, so choose a suitable vehicle.

Motorcycle Taxis:

Motorcycle taxis, known as "clandos," are a popular and efficient way to navigate through traffic, especially in busy urban areas. Negotiate the fare beforehand and ensure the availability of helmets for safety.

River Transportation:

In regions with waterways, such as the Bijagos Archipelago, boats and ferries are essential. Confirm schedules and safety measures before boarding. Some destinations may only be accessible by boat, so plan accordingly.

Navigation Apps and Maps:

While traditional paper maps are useful, consider using navigation apps to help you find your way. Make sure to download maps offline in case of limited internet connectivity, especially in rural areas.

Language Considerations:

English proficiency among local transportation providers may be limited, so it's beneficial to know some basic Portuguese phrases for communication. Additionally, writing down your destination or showing it on a map can be helpful.

Ask Locals for Guidance:
Locals are often friendly and willing to assist. If unsure about a transportation option or route, don't hesitate to ask for guidance. They can provide valuable insights and recommend the best means of getting to your destination.

Be Mindful of Peak Hours:
In urban areas, be aware of peak hours when traffic can be intense. Plan your journeys to avoid unnecessary delays, especially if you have time-sensitive plans or appointments.

Currency for Transportation:
Ensure you have small denominations of the local currency (West African CFA franc) for

transportation payments, as drivers may not always have change for larger bills.

By keeping these tips in mind, you can navigate Guinea-Bissau's local transportation systems with greater ease and make the most of your travel experience in this captivating West African country.

ACCOMMODATION OPTIONS

5.1 Overview of Accommodation Types

When embarking on a journey to Guinea-Bissau, the diverse range of accommodation options ensures that travelers can find lodging that suits their preferences, budget, and travel style. From bustling urban centers to serene coastal retreats, Guinea-Bissau offers a variety of places to stay, each contributing to a unique and immersive travel experience.

Hotels and Resorts:
- **Luxury Retreats:** Explore high-end hotels and resorts in Bissau and other major cities, offering top-notch amenities, world-class

service, and often featuring stunning views of the surrounding landscapes.

- **Mid-Range Comfort:** Discover comfortable and well-equipped mid-range hotels, providing a balance between affordability and quality services. These establishments cater to both business and leisure travelers.

Guesthouses and Inns:

- **Charming Guesthouses:** Immerse yourself in local hospitality by opting for guesthouses and inns scattered across Guinea-Bissau. These accommodations often offer a more intimate setting, personalized service, and a chance to connect with the local community.

- **Quaint Inns in Rural Areas:** Journey off the beaten path and find cozy inns in rural areas, providing an authentic experience in close proximity to nature and local traditions.

Eco-Lodges and Nature Retreats:

- **Bijagos Archipelago Retreats:** For those seeking an eco-friendly experience, consider staying at lodges on the Bijagos Archipelago. These accommodations blend seamlessly with the natural surroundings and provide an opportunity to appreciate Guinea-Bissau's biodiversity.

Budget Accommodations:

- **Hostels and Budget Guesthouses:** Ideal for budget-conscious travelers, hostels and budget guesthouses are available in major cities. They offer affordable lodging options without compromising on basic amenities.

Homestays and Community-Based Tourism:

- **Immersive Cultural Experiences:** Engage with local communities by choosing homestays or community-based tourism initiatives. These accommodations provide a unique opportunity to live with locals, learn about their daily lives, and contribute to sustainable tourism.

Beachfront Cabanas and Huts:

- **Seaside Retreats:** Along the coastal areas, discover beachfront cabanas and huts, allowing you to wake up to the sound of waves and enjoy the tranquility of Guinea-Bissau's pristine beaches.

Government Guesthouses:

- **Official Accommodations:** In certain regions, government guesthouses may be available for travelers. These options are often well-maintained and can offer a blend of comfort and affordability.

Camping and Outdoor Accommodations:

- **Nature Camping:** Explore the option of camping in designated areas, providing a more immersive experience for nature enthusiasts. Some accommodations offer tents or camping facilities for travelers looking to connect with Guinea-Bissau's natural beauty.

When planning your stay in Guinea-Bissau, consider the type of experience you seek, whether it be a luxurious retreat, an authentic cultural immersion, or a budget-friendly adventure. The variety of accommodation options ensures that every traveler can find the perfect place to call home during their exploration of this West African gem.

5.2 Recommendations for Budget, Mid-Range, and Luxury Stays

Guinea-Bissau offers a diverse range of accommodation options catering to different budgets and preferences. Whether you're a budget-conscious traveler, seeking mid-range comfort, or looking for luxury indulgence, the following recommendations will guide you to suitable accommodations across the country.

1. Budget Stays:

For travelers seeking economical options without compromising on comfort:

a. Pensão Residencial Chez Carneiro (Bissau):

- Centrally located budget accommodation with clean and simple rooms.
- Affordable rates and a friendly atmosphere.
- Close proximity to key attractions and local markets.

b. Bijagos Hostel (Bubaque Island, Bijagos Archipelago):

- Quaint hostel on Bubaque Island offering dormitory and private rooms.
- Ideal for budget travelers exploring the Bijagos Archipelago.
- Communal areas for socializing and sharing travel experiences.

c. Hotel Ancar (Bolama):

- Basic yet comfortable hotel in the historic town of Bolama.

- Affordable rates with a local charm.
- Convenient location for exploring Bolama Island.

2. Mid-Range Stays:

For travelers seeking a balance between comfort and cost:

a. Hotel Azalai 24 de Setembro (Bissau):

- Well-appointed mid-range hotel with modern amenities.
- Central location, making it convenient for both business and leisure travelers.
- On-site restaurant offering a mix of local and international cuisine.

b. Hotel Mar Azul (Bubaque Island, Bijagos Archipelago):

- Charming hotel overlooking the ocean on Bubaque Island.
- Comfortable rooms with sea views and a relaxing atmosphere.

- Proximity to Bubaque's attractions and beaches.

c. Hotel Orango en Bijagós (Orango Island):

- Mid-range hotel with a focus on eco-tourism.
- Serene surroundings and comfortable accommodations.
- Ideal for nature lovers exploring Orango Island.

3. Luxury Stays:

For travelers seeking premium accommodations and luxury amenities:

a. Hotel Ceiba (Bissau):

- Five-star hotel offering luxurious rooms and suites.
- Elegant design, modern facilities, and personalized service.
- Fine dining options and a rooftop bar with panoramic views.

b. Djurtus Hotel (Bubaque Island, Bijagos Archipelago):

- Boutique luxury hotel with a tranquil setting on Bubaque Island.
- Spacious suites, private terraces, and personalized services.
- Private beach access and a spa for ultimate relaxation.

c. Bijagós Palace Hotel (Bolama):

- Historical luxury hotel set in a colonial-era building in Bolama.
- Lavishly decorated rooms, gourmet dining, and a sophisticated ambiance.
- Unique blend of history and modern luxury.

Note: Prices and availability may vary, and it's advisable to check with the respective hotels for the latest information. Additionally, booking in advance, especially during peak seasons, is recommended for a smoother travel experience.

5.3 Unique Lodging Experiences

When exploring Guinea-Bissau, your accommodation can be an integral part of the adventure. Experience the charm and authenticity of the country by considering these unique lodging options:

1. Ecolodges in the Bijagos Archipelago:

- Immerse yourself in nature by staying at one of the eco-friendly lodges in the Bijagos Archipelago. These establishments prioritize sustainability, offering a close connection to the surrounding environment.
- Enjoy the sounds of nature, breathtaking views, and a chance to witness local wildlife in their natural habitat.

2. Community Homestays in Rural Villages:

- For a truly immersive experience, consider staying with local families in rural villages. Several community-based initiatives offer homestays, allowing travelers to engage directly with the culture and daily life of the people.

- Participate in traditional activities, share meals, and gain insights into the authentic Bissau-Guinean way of life.

3. Floating Bungalows on the Cacheu River:

- Experience tranquility and unique riverfront living by choosing a floating bungalow on the Cacheu River. These accommodations provide a peaceful escape surrounded by the natural beauty of mangroves and riverine landscapes.

- Ideal for those seeking serenity and a one-of-a-kind stay off the beaten path.

4. Historical Boutique Hotels in Bissau City:

- Discover the charm of colonial-era buildings transformed into boutique hotels in Bissau City. These establishments blend history with modern amenities, offering a unique and comfortable stay.

- Enjoy the architectural beauty of well-preserved structures while being centrally located for easy exploration of the capital.

5. Beachfront Cabanas in Varela:

- Varela, known for its pristine beaches, offers beachfront cabanas for a laid-back and idyllic retreat. Wake up to the sound of waves, take leisurely walks on the beach, and witness stunning sunsets from the comfort of your own private cabana.

- Perfect for those seeking a romantic getaway or a peaceful escape from the hustle and bustle.

6. Island Retreats in Orango:

- Orango Island, part of the Bijagos Archipelago, boasts exclusive island retreats. These secluded accommodations provide an intimate setting with personalized services, ensuring a luxurious and private escape.

- Enjoy the beauty of untouched beaches, indulge in gourmet cuisine, and relax in a tranquil paradise.

Choosing one of these unique lodging experiences will not only enhance your stay in Guinea-Bissau but also contribute to sustainable and community-focused tourism, creating lasting memories of your journey in this West African gem.

CULTURAL ETIQUETTE AND CUSTOMS

6.1 Dos and Don'ts in Guinea-Bissau

Guinea-Bissau, with its rich cultural tapestry and unique traditions, offers travelers a fascinating experience. To ensure a smooth and respectful journey, it's essential to be aware of the dos and don'ts in Guinea-Bissau. Understanding local customs will not only enrich your experience but also contribute to positive interactions with the warm and welcoming locals.

Dos:

Greet with Respect:

- Greetings are important in Guinea-Bissau. When meeting someone, a warm handshake and a simple greeting in Portuguese, the official language, are appreciated.

Ask for Permission to Take Photos:

- Before taking pictures of people, especially in rural areas, ask for permission. Many locals may appreciate the courtesy and enjoy participating in the experience.

Respect Traditional Customs:

- Guinea-Bissau has a rich cultural heritage. Respect local customs, ceremonies, and traditions. If attending an event, follow the lead of locals and adhere to any guidelines.

Dress Modestly:

- In urban areas and religious sites, it's advisable to dress modestly. Women, in particular, may want to avoid revealing clothing out of respect for local norms.

Use Right Hand for Gestures:

- When giving or receiving something, always use your right hand. The left hand is traditionally considered less clean in many West African cultures.

Haggle Politely:

- Bargaining is common in markets. When negotiating prices, do so with a friendly and respectful attitude. It's part of the local culture, and a little haggling is expected.

Be Open to Communication:

- Embrace conversations with locals. The people of Guinea-Bissau are known for their friendliness. Engaging in simple conversations can lead to valuable insights into the local way of life.

Remove Shoes Indoors:

- When entering someone's home, it's customary to remove your shoes. This practice is a sign of respect for the household.

Be Mindful of Elders:

- Show deference to older individuals in the community. Use polite language and gestures when interacting with elders.

Support Local Businesses:

- Opt for locally-owned shops, restaurants, and accommodations to contribute to the community's economic well-being.

Don'ts:

Don't Disrespect Religious Sites:

- Avoid loud conversations and disruptive behavior at religious sites. Always ask for permission before taking pictures in or around places of worship.

Don't Engage in Public Displays of Affection:

- Public displays of affection are not common in Guinea-Bissau. It's advisable to keep such gestures private out of respect for local cultural norms.

Avoid Negative Gestures:

- Pointing with fingers is considered impolite. Instead, use your whole hand to gesture or beckon.

Don't Litter:

- Maintain environmental responsibility by disposing of trash properly. Keep the environment clean, and avoid littering in public spaces.

Refrain from Discussing Politics Intensely:

- While casual discussions about politics are acceptable, avoid engaging in intense or controversial political debates, as this can be sensitive.

Don't Enter Homes Uninvited:

- Always wait for an invitation before entering someone's home. It's a common courtesy to respect the privacy of others.

Avoid Negative Comments about Culture:

- Refrain from making negative comments about local customs or traditions. Instead, seek to understand and appreciate the cultural diversity.

By keeping these dos and don'ts in mind, you'll not only navigate Guinea-Bissau more smoothly but also contribute to positive cross-cultural interactions, fostering a deeper connection with this vibrant West African nation.

6.2 Traditional Customs and Festivals in Guinea-Bissau

Guinea-Bissau is a vibrant and culturally rich country with a tapestry of traditional customs and festivals that reflect the diversity of its ethnic groups. Understanding and participating in these celebrations offer travelers a unique insight into the local way of life. Here's a detailed exploration of some of Guinea-Bissau's significant traditions and festivals:

Tabaski (Eid al-Adha):

- Celebrated by the Muslim community, Tabaski is one of the most important religious festivals in Guinea-Bissau.
- It marks the end of the Hajj pilgrimage and commemorates the willingness of Ibrahim (Abraham) to sacrifice his son as an act of obedience to God.

- Families come together for prayers, feasts, and the exchange of gifts. It's a time of charity and compassion.

Festival de Bubaque:

- Held annually on Bubaque Island in the Bijagos Archipelago, this cultural festival showcases traditional music, dance, and rituals of the Bijagós people.
- Visitors can witness traditional mask dances, ceremonies honoring ancestral spirits, and displays of traditional craftsmanship.
- The festival provides a unique opportunity to immerse oneself in the vibrant cultural heritage of the Bijagós.

Carnival in Bissau:

- The Carnival in Bissau is a lively and colorful celebration that takes place before Lent.
- Locals and visitors alike participate in parades, wearing elaborate costumes and

masks, accompanied by traditional music and dance.

- It's a time of joy, music, and socializing, with the streets coming alive with energy and enthusiasm.

Fanado Ceremony:

- The Fanado is a rite of passage ceremony among the Balanta people, symbolizing the transition from adolescence to adulthood.
- The ceremony involves elaborate rituals, traditional dances, and the donning of special costumes.
- It's a deeply spiritual event, and travelers may have the opportunity to witness aspects of this sacred tradition with the Balanta community.

New Year's Eve Celebrations:

- New Year's Eve is a festive occasion celebrated with enthusiasm and joy throughout Guinea-Bissau.

- Local communities gather for music, dance, and fireworks, creating a lively atmosphere to welcome the new year.
- Travelers can join in the festivities, enjoying the warmth and hospitality of the locals.

Dipana Dance Festival:

- The Dipana Dance Festival, celebrated by the Bijagós people, is a unique cultural event where masked dancers perform to honor the spirits.
- The festival includes traditional ceremonies, music, and dance, providing an immersive experience into the spiritual beliefs of the Bijagós.

Initiation Ceremonies:

- Various ethnic groups in Guinea-Bissau, such as the Manjaco and Pepel, conduct initiation ceremonies for young individuals.

- These ceremonies involve rituals, dance performances, and communal feasts, symbolizing the passage into adulthood.
- While access to these ceremonies may be limited, respectful engagement may allow travelers to observe certain aspects.

Participating in or observing these traditional customs and festivals provides travelers with a deeper appreciation for Guinea-Bissau's cultural richness and the warmth of its people. It's essential to approach these events with respect and an open mind, embracing the opportunity to connect with the local communities on a profound level.

6.3 Dress Code and Cultural Sensitivities in Guinea-Bissau

Understanding and respecting the local dress code and cultural sensitivities is crucial for travelers to have a positive and culturally immersive experience in Guinea-Bissau. The country's cultural diversity is reflected in its people's clothing traditions, and adhering to certain norms will contribute to a more harmonious interaction with the local population. Here's a detailed guide:

Casual Attire:

- Guinea-Bissau has a generally relaxed approach to clothing, especially in urban areas. Casual and comfortable clothing is suitable for most situations. Light, breathable fabrics are advisable due to the tropical climate.

Respectful Covering:

- While casual attire is accepted, it's important to ensure that clothing covers essential body parts, particularly when visiting religious sites or rural communities. Women may want to carry a shawl or scarf for added coverage when needed.

Beachwear and Modesty:

- Beachwear is appropriate at the beach, but wearing it in other public places is considered inappropriate. When leaving the beach, it's recommended to change into more modest clothing to show respect for local customs.

Traditional Attire:

- Embrace the opportunity to experience Guinea-Bissau's rich cultural heritage by participating in traditional events or ceremonies. Wearing traditional attire, such as colorful fabrics and prints, can be a sign of appreciation and respect.

Religious Sites:

- When visiting mosques or other religious sites, both men and women should dress modestly. Women may need to cover their heads, and it's advisable to wear long skirts or pants.

Footwear:

- As a sign of respect, it's customary to remove shoes when entering someone's home. It's also practical to wear comfortable and durable footwear, especially if exploring rural areas.

Tattoos and Body Art:

- While tattoos are becoming more accepted, some traditional communities may still view them with skepticism. It's advisable to cover tattoos when visiting such areas, especially in rural villages.

Greeting Customs:

- Understanding local greeting customs is also part of cultural sensitivity. In some communities, a handshake or a nod is appropriate, while in others, a more elaborate greeting ritual might be expected.

Photography Etiquette:

- Always seek permission before taking photographs, especially of individuals. Some people may have cultural or religious reasons for not wanting their picture taken.

LGBTQ+ Considerations:

- Guinea-Bissau is relatively tolerant, but public displays of affection, regardless of sexual orientation, may be viewed with reserve. It's advisable to be discreet in this regard.

By being mindful of the local dress code and cultural sensitivities, travelers can build positive connections with the people of Guinea-Bissau and fully appreciate the rich cultural tapestry that makes the country unique. Respect and understanding go a long way in creating meaningful and authentic travel experiences.

EXPLORING REGIONS AND CITIES

7.1 Bissau City: Capital Highlights

Bissau, the capital city of Guinea-Bissau, is a vibrant and culturally rich destination that offers a diverse range of experiences for travelers. This section of the travel guide delves into the key highlights of Bissau City, providing insights into its history, landmarks, cultural attractions, and local charm.

Historical Significance:

Explore the historical roots of Bissau City, including its colonial past and struggle for independence. Visit key landmarks such as the Pidjiguiti Memorial, which commemorates the 1959 dockworkers' strike that played a pivotal role in the country's fight for freedom.

Bissau Velho (Old Bissau):

Wander through the narrow streets of Bissau Velho, the historic district, where colonial-era architecture and colorful buildings create a charming atmosphere. Visit the Presidential Palace and the National Ethnographic Museum to gain insights into the city's past.

Bandim Market:

Immerse yourself in the vibrant atmosphere of Bandim Market, one of the largest and liveliest markets in West Africa. Experience the local culture as you browse through stalls selling fresh produce, traditional crafts, and a variety of goods. Engage with friendly vendors and savor the flavors of local street food.

Bolama Island:

Take a short boat ride to Bolama Island, the former capital of Portuguese Guinea. Explore the remnants of colonial architecture, including the impressive Governor's Palace and the Cathedral. The island offers a tranquil escape with its serene beaches and historical allure.

Guinea-Bissau National Arts Institute:
Delve into the country's rich artistic heritage at the National Arts Institute in Bissau. Discover traditional music, dance, and visual arts that showcase the diversity of Guinea-Bissau's cultural expressions. Attend live performances and exhibitions to appreciate the local talent.

Guinea-Bissau National Museum:
Visit the National Museum to gain a deeper understanding of the country's history and cultural evolution. The museum houses artifacts, documents, and exhibits that trace Guinea-Bissau's journey from pre-colonial times to the present day.

Independence Plaza:
Witness the heartbeat of Bissau City at Independence Plaza, a central square surrounded by government buildings and monuments. The statue

of Amilcar Cabral, a key figure in the country's independence movement, stands tall, symbolizing the nation's struggle for freedom.

Cuisine and Nightlife:
Experience the local gastronomy at Bissau's diverse restaurants, offering a blend of Portuguese and African flavors. As night falls, explore the city's nightlife scene, where lively bars and clubs provide opportunities to mingle with locals and fellow travelers.

Bissau City, with its historical significance, vibrant markets, and cultural landmarks, offers a captivating blend of tradition and modernity. This section of the travel guide encourages travelers to explore the heart of Guinea-Bissau and appreciate the unique character of its capital.

7.2 Bijagos Archipelago: Natural Wonders

Overview:

The Bijagos Archipelago, situated off the coast of Guinea-Bissau in the Atlantic Ocean, is a captivating collection of islands renowned for their natural beauty, diverse ecosystems, and unique cultural heritage. Comprising approximately 88 islands, the archipelago is a UNESCO Biosphere Reserve, recognized for its rich biodiversity and the preservation of traditional Bijagó culture.

Geography and Islands:
Bolama Island:

- The largest island in the archipelago and a former colonial capital.
- Historical sites, including abandoned colonial-era buildings and Bolama's distinct charm.

Bubaque Island:

- The most populous and a hub for cultural experiences.

- Traditional Bijagó villages, vibrant markets, and opportunities to engage with local communities.

Orango Island:
- A significant wildlife sanctuary with a diverse ecosystem.
- Home to saltwater hippos, sea turtles, and numerous bird species.
- The sacred Orango Grande, a site of traditional ceremonies.

João Vieira and Poilão Marine National Park:
- A protected area encompassing several islands, known for its marine biodiversity.
- Rich marine life, including dolphins, manatees, and various fish species.

Natural Attractions:
Beaches and Coastlines:
- Pristine, unspoiled beaches with golden sands and crystal-clear waters.

- Ideal for relaxation, water activities, and bird watching.

Mangrove Forests:
- Extensive mangrove ecosystems, vital for the archipelago's ecological balance.
- Guided tours showcasing the unique flora and fauna of the mangroves.

Wildlife Encounters:
- Opportunities for bird watching, with over 200 bird species recorded.
- Observation of sea turtles nesting and hatching on designated beaches.

Cultural Experiences:
Bijagó Culture:
- Interaction with the indigenous Bijagó people, known for their rich cultural traditions.
- Participation in traditional ceremonies, dances, and rituals.

Art and Crafts:

- Authentic Bijagó handicrafts, including wood carvings, masks, and vibrant textiles.
- Local artisans' workshops showcasing traditional craftsmanship.

Activities and Exploration:

Boat Tours and Island Hopping:

- Exploring the archipelago's islands by boat, offering stunning panoramic views.
- Visits to various islands, each with its own unique charm and attractions.

Diving and Snorkeling:

- Rich underwater biodiversity, with coral reefs and marine life.
- Dive centers providing equipment and guided excursions.

Logistics:

Access:

- Transportation options from Bissau to the archipelago, including boat services and occasional flights.
- Timings and schedules for transportation services.

Accommodation:
- Lodging options on major islands, ranging from eco-friendly resorts to guesthouses.
- Booking considerations and availability.

Conservation and Responsible Tourism:
Preservation Efforts:
- UNESCO Biosphere Reserve designation and ongoing conservation initiatives.
- Guidelines for responsible tourism to minimize environmental impact.

Visiting the Bijagos Archipelago offers a rare opportunity to connect with nature, experience vibrant local cultures, and contribute to the preservation of this ecologically significant region.

Whether seeking adventure, cultural immersion, or simply relaxation, the archipelago stands as one of Guinea-Bissau's foremost natural wonders.

7.3 Regions Off the Beaten Path

Guinea-Bissau is not just about its capital city; there are hidden gems in lesser-explored regions that offer a more authentic and off-the-beaten-path experience for intrepid travelers. Delve into the undiscovered beauty of these regions:

1. Cacheu Region

Nestled History and Natural Tranquility

- **Historical Landmarks:** Explore the historic city of Cacheu, known for its colonial architecture and the remnants of Fort Cacheu, which played a crucial role in the slave trade.

- **Rio Cacheu:** Embark on a serene boat trip along the Rio Cacheu, witnessing lush mangroves, diverse bird species, and traditional fishing villages lining its banks.

- **Community Encounters:** Engage with local communities, such as the Manjaco people, known for their vibrant cultural practices and traditional beliefs.

2. Gabú Region
Untouched Wilderness and Ethnic Diversity

- **Landscape Diversity:** Discover the diverse landscapes of Gabú, ranging from savannahs to dense forests, creating a haven for nature enthusiasts.
- **Léléwa Forest:** Immerse yourself in the Léléwa Forest, home to unique flora and fauna, and connect with local guides to gain insights into traditional healing practices.
- **Ethnic Villages:** Visit ethnic villages like the Balanta and Felupe, known for their traditional rituals, music, and dance, offering a glimpse into Guinea-Bissau's cultural tapestry.

3. Quinara Region
Coastal Charm and Fishing Communities

- **Buba and the Archipelago:** Explore the coastal town of Buba, a gateway to the Bijagos Archipelago, and embark on boat excursions to discover untouched islands and pristine beaches.
- **Bijagos Culture:** Encounter the Bijagos people, known for their unique cultural practices and ancient mask ceremonies, providing an authentic cultural experience.
- **Fishing Communities:** Engage with local fishing communities, witnessing traditional fishing techniques and enjoying freshly caught seafood prepared in traditional styles.

4. Oio Region

Rural Landscapes and Agricultural Traditions

- **Agricultural Heartland:** Visit the Oio Region to witness Guinea-Bissau's agricultural heartland, with vast expanses of rice paddies and cashew plantations.
- **Tchon:** Explore the rural town of Tchon, known for its traditional round houses, and

experience the warmth of the local hospitality.

- **Local Markets:** Wander through local markets, such as Farim Market, where you can witness the daily life of the locals and discover handmade crafts and agricultural produce.

Exploring these off-the-beaten-path regions provides a unique opportunity to connect with Guinea-Bissau's rich cultural diversity, unspoiled landscapes, and the warmth of its welcoming communities, making for an unforgettable travel experience.

HISTORICAL AND CULTURAL LANDMARKS

8.1 Fortaleza d'Amura: Exploring Guinea-Bissau's Historical Fortress

Fortaleza d'Amura, located in Bissau, the capital city of Guinea-Bissau, stands as a testament to the country's rich historical past. This historical fortress, also known as Fortaleza de São José da Amura, holds a significant place in Guinea-Bissau's history and offers visitors a glimpse into the colonial era.

Historical Significance:

Constructed in the late 18th century by the Portuguese, Fortaleza d'Amura served as a strategic military stronghold during the colonial period. Its primary purpose was to safeguard the city and its inhabitants from potential invasions and attacks. Over the years, the fortress played a crucial role in the region's history, witnessing various colonial struggles and socio-political changes.

Architectural Features:

The architecture of Fortaleza d'Amura reflects a blend of European military design and local influences. The fortress is characterized by sturdy stone walls, watchtowers, and cannons strategically positioned to defend against maritime threats. Visitors can explore the various sections of the fortress, including the central courtyard, historical rooms, and the commanding views from the top of the walls.

Museum and Exhibits:

Today, Fortaleza d'Amura houses a museum that showcases artifacts and exhibits related to Guinea-Bissau's colonial history. Visitors can view colonial-era weaponry, documents, and displays providing insight into the daily life of the soldiers stationed at the fortress. The museum aims to educate visitors about the cultural and historical heritage of Guinea-Bissau.

Panoramic Views:

One of the highlights of visiting Fortaleza d'Amura is the panoramic view it offers of Bissau and the surrounding areas. From the elevated vantage points within the fortress, visitors can enjoy breathtaking views of the cityscape, the Geba River, and the Atlantic Ocean.

Visiting Tips:

- **Opening Hours:** Check the current opening hours as they may vary.
- **Guided Tours:** Engage with knowledgeable local guides who can provide historical insights.
- **Photography:** Capture the scenic views and historical details, but be mindful of any photography restrictions.
- **Footwear:** Wear comfortable shoes, especially if exploring the walls and towers.

Getting There:

Fortaleza d'Amura is conveniently located in the heart of Bissau, making it easily accessible for tourists. Most accommodations in the city can provide directions, and local transportation options, such as taxis, are readily available.

A visit to Fortaleza d'Amura offers not only a journey into Guinea-Bissau's past but also a chance to appreciate the architectural and historical richness of the region. Whether you are a history enthusiast or a traveler seeking cultural experiences, exploring Fortaleza d'Amura is a must for an enriching and educational visit to Guinea-Bissau.

8.2 Bolama Island: Unveiling the Historic Heart of Guinea-Bissau

Bolama Island, located off the coast of Guinea-Bissau, is a hidden gem that captivates visitors with its rich history, colonial charm, and picturesque landscapes. Once the capital of Portuguese Guinea, Bolama holds a unique position as a testament to the nation's past, making it a must-visit destination for travelers seeking cultural insights and serene beauty.

Historical Significance:

- **Colonial Legacy:** Bolama served as the capital of Portuguese Guinea from 1871 to 1941, leaving behind a legacy of colonial architecture and historic structures. Explore remnants of this era, including government buildings and colonial-era residences.

- **Pidjiguiti Memorial:** The island is also known for the Pidjiguiti Memorial, commemorating the 1959 dockworker strike that played a pivotal role in the fight against Portuguese colonial rule. The memorial stands as a symbol of the nation's struggle for independence.

Landmarks and Points of Interest:

- **Bolama Palácio:** Visit the Bolama Palácio, a once-grand presidential palace, now in a state of picturesque decay. Its faded grandeur tells stories of a bygone era, and the surrounding gardens offer a peaceful retreat.

- **Catedral Nossa Senhora da Candelária:** Discover the historic Catedral Nossa Senhora da Candelária, a cathedral dating back to the late 19th century. The cathedral's architecture reflects a blend of European and local influences.

- **Bolama Bungalow:** Explore the Bolama Bungalow, a charming guesthouse that provides an authentic experience. The bungalow is an excellent base for visitors keen on immersing themselves in Bolama's unique atmosphere.

Natural Beauty:

- **Mangrove Swamps:** Bolama Island boasts extensive mangrove swamps, providing a habitat for diverse bird species. Birdwatchers will delight in the opportunity to observe native and migratory birds in their natural surroundings.

- **Scenic Beaches:** Enjoy the tranquility of Bolama's pristine beaches, where azure waters meet golden sands. Ideal for relaxation, these beaches offer a serene escape from the hustle and bustle.

Practical Tips:

- **Getting There:** Bolama Island is accessible by boat from Bissau, and regular ferry services connect the mainland to the island. It's advisable to check the ferry schedules in advance.

- **Accommodation:** While accommodation options on Bolama are limited, the Bolama Bungalow provides a unique and authentic stay. Visitors should consider booking in advance, especially during peak travel seasons.

- **Local Cuisine:** Experience local flavors with seafood delicacies at small eateries on the island. Engage with locals to discover traditional dishes that showcase the region's culinary heritage.

Bolama Island stands as a living museum, inviting travelers to delve into the pages of Guinea-Bissau's history while basking in the island's natural beauty. Whether fascinated by colonial architecture, intrigued by historical narratives, or seeking serene landscapes, Bolama promises a truly enriching experience for every explorer.

8.3 Pidjiguiti Memorial: A Tribute to Guinea-Bissau's Struggle for Independence

The Pidjiguiti Memorial, situated in the heart of Bissau, serves as a poignant reminder of Guinea-Bissau's relentless fight for independence from Portuguese colonial rule. This memorial holds immense historical significance, commemorating a pivotal moment in the nation's quest for freedom.

Historical Background:

Built on the grounds of the Pidjiguiti Dockworkers' Strike that transpired on August 3, 1959, the memorial pays homage to the workers who protested poor conditions, unknowingly sparking a movement that played a crucial role in Guinea-Bissau's liberation.

Architecture and Design:

Symbolic in design, the memorial features a powerful sculpture depicting a fist breaking through chains, representing the nation's break from colonial oppression. The architecture incorporates elements of local culture, emphasizing unity and strength.

Visiting the Memorial:

- **Exhibition Hall:** Delve into the on-site exhibition hall, featuring a comprehensive historical overview through photographs, artifacts, and informative displays that shed light on the events leading to the strike and its aftermath.

- **The Strike Grounds:** Explore the preserved Pidjiguiti Dock, where the historic strike unfolded. Plaques and markers guide visitors through the key locations, enabling them to retrace the steps of the courageous workers.

- **Memorial Square:** The surrounding square serves as a gathering place for both locals and visitors, often hosting events, discussions, and cultural activities, fostering a sense of community and remembrance.

Educational and Cultural Significance:

The Pidjiguiti Memorial acts as an invaluable educational resource, enlightening visitors about the sacrifices made by those who fought for Guinea-Bissau's freedom. It also plays a crucial role in preserving the nation's cultural identity, ensuring that future generations understand the struggles that shaped their country.

Practical Information:

- **Location:** Bairro Bandim, Bissau, Guinea-Bissau

Opening Hours:

- **Monday to Saturday: 9:00 AM to 5:00 PM**
- **Sundays:** Closed

Admission Fees:

- **Adults**: [Specify fee]
- **Children (under 12):** [Specify fee]
- **Students (with valid ID):** [Specify fee]

A visit to the Pidjiguiti Memorial not only offers a historical journey but also provides an opportunity to pay homage to the resilience and courage of the Guinean people. It stands as a powerful reminder of the nation's struggle for independence and the enduring spirit that continues to shape Guinea-Bissau's identity

8.4 Bandim Market: A Vibrant Tapestry of Guinea-Bissau's Culture and Commerce

Bandim Market, located in the heart of Bissau, the capital city of Guinea-Bissau, stands as a bustling testament to the rich cultural tapestry and vibrant commerce that defines this West African nation. As one of the largest and most vibrant markets in the country, Bandim Market offers a sensory journey through the sights, sounds, and flavors of Guinea-Bissau.

Historical Significance:

Dating back to colonial times, Bandim Market has evolved from a modest trading post to a thriving marketplace that reflects the historical, social, and economic dynamics of the region. The market has weathered the tides of time, witnessing the country's journey to independence and becoming a symbol of resilience and community spirit.

Location:

Nestled within the labyrinthine streets of Bissau, Bandim Market serves as a central hub for locals and visitors alike. Its strategic location makes it easily accessible, and the market's vibrancy spills into the surrounding areas, creating a lively atmosphere.

Diversity of Goods:

Bandim Market is a treasure trove for those seeking an authentic Guinea-Bissau experience. The market is a kaleidoscope of colors and textures, offering a diverse range of goods. Visitors can explore stalls filled with fresh produce, traditional textiles, handicrafts, spices, and an array of local products that showcase the country's rich cultural heritage.

Local Cuisine and Delicacies:

One of the highlights of Bandim Market is the tantalizing array of local cuisine. Food stalls and vendors offer a mouthwatering selection of traditional dishes, providing an opportunity for visitors to savor the flavors of Guinea-Bissau. From aromatic spices to exotic fruits, the market is a culinary adventure waiting to be explored.

Interacting with Locals:
Bandim Market provides a unique opportunity to engage with the warm and welcoming locals. Vendors often share stories about their products, offer cooking tips, and provide insights into the cultural significance of various items. This interaction adds a personal touch to the shopping experience and enhances the cultural immersion for visitors.

Tips for Visitors:
- **Timing:** Visit the market in the morning for the liveliest atmosphere and the freshest produce.
- **Bargaining:** Bargaining is a customary practice, and friendly negotiations are part of the market experience.

- **Respect Local Customs:** Be mindful of local customs and seek permission before taking photographs.

Bandim Market encapsulates the spirit of Guinea-Bissau, offering a dynamic and authentic experience for travelers. Whether you're seeking unique souvenirs, sampling local delicacies, or simply immersing yourself in the vibrant atmosphere, a visit to Bandim Market is an essential part of any Guinea-Bissau itinerary.

OUTDOOR ADVENTURE AND NATURE

9.1 Bijagos National Marine Park: A Natural Paradise in Guinea-Bissau

Nestled along the Atlantic coastline of Guinea-Bissau, the Bijagos National Marine Park stands as a testament to the country's rich biodiversity and natural beauty. This protected area, declared a national park in 1996, encompasses a unique archipelago of islands in the Bijagos Archipelago. The park is a haven for wildlife enthusiasts, ecotourists, and those seeking an unspoiled natural escape.

Geography and Islands:
The Bijagos National Marine Park covers an extensive area, consisting of approximately 88 islands and islets. The archipelago is renowned for its diverse landscapes, ranging from pristine

beaches and mangrove swamps to dense forests and savannahs. Notable islands within the park include Orango, João Vieira, Poilão, and Uno.

Wildlife Sanctuary:

One of the primary draws of the Bijagos National Marine Park is its status as a vital wildlife sanctuary. The park is home to a remarkable array of flora and fauna, including rare and endangered species. Visitors have the opportunity to witness diverse marine life, such as sea turtles, dolphins, and manatees, while the surrounding islands provide habitats for numerous bird species, including pelicans and flamingos.

Sea Turtle Conservation:

The Bijagos Archipelago is a crucial nesting ground for sea turtles, particularly the endangered loggerhead and green turtles. Conservation efforts within the marine park focus on protecting these nesting sites and ensuring the survival of the turtle populations. Travelers can participate in guided tours to witness nesting activities and learn about the conservation initiatives in place.

Orango Island: A Jewel in the Archipelago:
Orango Island, a highlight of the Bijagos National Marine Park, captivates visitors with its lush landscapes and cultural significance. The island is home to the Bijagos people, and visitors can explore traditional villages, witness vibrant ceremonies, and immerse themselves in the local way of life. Orango also hosts a wildlife sanctuary dedicated to the protection of hippos, crocodiles, and numerous bird species.

Activities and Exploration:
- **Nature Walks and Hiking:** Explore the diverse ecosystems of the islands through guided nature walks and hikes, led by knowledgeable local guides.
- **Bird Watching:** With over 200 bird species recorded, the park is a paradise for bird

watchers. Binoculars in hand, visitors can spot both resident and migratory birds.

- **Boat Tours and Island Hopping:** Discover the archipelago's hidden gems with boat tours that navigate the crystal-clear waters, stopping at different islands for unique experiences.

- **Cultural Experiences:** Engage with the Bijagos people, learn about their traditions, and witness vibrant ceremonies that provide insight into the archipelago's rich cultural heritage.

Practical Information:

- **Best Time to Visit:** The dry season from November to April is ideal for wildlife observation and outdoor activities.

- **Permit and Fees:** Entry to the Bijagos National Marine Park may require a permit, and fees contribute to conservation efforts.

- **Accommodation:** While accommodations on the islands may be limited, nearby mainland options are available for visitors.

The Bijagos National Marine Park is a true gem in Guinea-Bissau, offering a harmonious blend of nature, wildlife, and cultural richness for those seeking an authentic and unforgettable travel experience.

9.2 Forests and Natural Reserves in Guinea-Bissau

Guinea-Bissau is a country blessed with diverse ecosystems, and its forests and natural reserves offer a haven for nature enthusiasts and those seeking a unique and immersive experience. Here is a detailed exploration of the lush greenery and pristine landscapes found within Guinea-Bissau:

Bijagos National Marine Park:
Location: Western Guinea-Bissau, covering the Bijagos Archipelago.

Overview: A UNESCO Biosphere Reserve, Bijagos National Marine Park is a jewel in Guinea-Bissau's natural crown. The park encompasses a network of islands, mangroves, and marine habitats, providing refuge to a rich array of wildlife.

Highlights:

- **Biodiversity:** Discover an impressive variety of marine life, including dolphins, sea turtles, and diverse fish species.

- **Island Sanctuaries:** Explore individual islands within the archipelago, each with its unique ecosystems and bird species.

- **Cultural Significance:** Engage with local communities residing on some of the islands, known for their traditional customs and rituals.

Orango Island: Wildlife Sanctuary:

Location: Orango Island, part of the Bijagos Archipelago.

Overview: Orango Island stands out as a wildlife sanctuary and a place of natural beauty. The island's unique blend of ecosystems makes it a haven for both terrestrial and marine species.

Highlights:

- **Saltwater Hippopotamuses:** Witness the rare presence of saltwater hippos, a unique phenomenon found in Guinea-Bissau.
- **Bird Watching:** Orango is a paradise for bird enthusiasts, with a multitude of species gracing its skies and shores.
- **Mangrove Forests:** Explore the intricate mangrove ecosystems, vital for the conservation of various marine life.

Cantanhez Forest and Natural Reserve:

Location: Southeastern Guinea-Bissau, near the town of Catió.

Overview: The Cantanhez Forest and Natural Reserve is a terrestrial counterpart to the marine wonders of the Bijagos Archipelago. This reserve is a testament to Guinea-Bissau's commitment to preserving its natural heritage.

Highlights:

- **Primate Conservation:** Encounter rare primates, including the endangered chimpanzees and Guinea baboons, in their natural habitat.
- **Flora Diversity:** Immerse yourself in the rich diversity of plant life, from towering trees to vibrant orchids.
- **Hiking Trails:** Enjoy well-maintained trails that lead you through the heart of the forest, offering glimpses of its hidden treasures.

João Vieira and Poilão Marine National Park:

Location: Off the coast of Guinea-Bissau, comprising João Vieira Island, Poilão Island, and several smaller islets.

Overview: This marine national park is renowned for its pristine coral reefs, abundant marine life, and the conservation of endangered species.

Highlights:

- **Marine Conservation:** Dive or snorkel to witness vibrant coral reefs and an array of marine species, contributing to the park's conservation efforts.

- **Sea Turtle Nesting:** Experience the awe-inspiring sight of sea turtles nesting on the beaches of João Vieira Island.
- **Guided Boat Tours:** Explore the park with knowledgeable guides who provide insights into its ecological importance and conservation initiatives.

Exploring Guinea-Bissau's forests and natural reserves offers a captivating blend of biodiversity, cultural richness, and pristine landscapes, making it an essential component of any traveler's itinerary in this West African gem.

LOCAL CUISINE AND DINNING

10.1 Traditional Dishes and Culinary Highlights in Guinea-Bissau

Guinea-Bissau's culinary scene is a delightful blend of flavors influenced by its African, Portuguese, and indigenous cultures. The rich diversity of seafood, tropical fruits, and aromatic spices make the country's traditional dishes a unique and memorable experience for any traveler. Here's a detailed exploration of the traditional dishes and culinary highlights you should savor during your visit:

Bafas:

- **Description:** Bafas is a popular dish in Guinea-Bissau, consisting of fish or meat cooked in a flavorful sauce made with palm oil, onions, tomatoes, and various spices. It is often served with rice or couscous.

Caldo de Mancarra:

- **Description:** This is a hearty groundnut stew that typically includes chicken, fish, or meat, along with vegetables like okra and spinach. Groundnuts (peanuts) provide a creamy texture and nutty flavor to the dish.

Arroz de Jollof:

- **Description:** Arroz de Jollof is a West African dish, and in Guinea-Bissau, it is a popular rice dish cooked with tomatoes, onions, and various spices. It is often served with grilled or stewed fish, chicken, or meat.

Funge and Fish Soup:

- **Description:** Funge is a starchy dish made from cassava or rice flour, resembling a soft and sticky dough. It is often paired with a rich fish soup, creating a comforting and satisfying meal.

Akara:

- **Description:** Akara is a popular street food made from ground black-eyed peas formed into deep-fried fritters. These savory snacks are enjoyed throughout the day and are often served with spicy pepper sauce.

Amilcar Cabral Soup:

- **Description:** Named after the national hero, Amilcar Cabral Soup is a flavorful soup made with a variety of vegetables, fish, and sometimes meat. It reflects the country's appreciation for fresh, locally sourced ingredients.

Canja de Galinha:

- **Description:** This is a comforting chicken soup made with rice, vegetables, and aromatic herbs. Canja de Galinha is often served during special occasions and celebrations, providing warmth and nourishment.

Cashew Nut Liquor:

- **Description:** Guinea-Bissau is known for its cashew production, and cashew nut liquor is a popular alcoholic beverage. It features the distinct taste of cashews and is enjoyed as a digestive or aperitif.

Pirão:

- **Description:** Pirão is a porridge-like dish made from the broth of fish or meat. Cassava flour is added to thicken the mixture, creating a hearty accompaniment to grilled or stewed dishes.

Fruit Delights:

- **Description:** Guinea-Bissau boasts an abundance of tropical fruits. Try the sweet and refreshing flavors of mangoes, guavas, pineapples, and bananas, either as standalone treats or incorporated into various dishes and desserts.

Exploring Guinea-Bissau's traditional dishes provides not only a gastronomic adventure but also a deeper understanding of the country's cultural richness. Don't miss the opportunity to indulge in these culinary delights and savor the unique tastes that make Guinea-Bissau a remarkable destination for food enthusiasts.

10.2 Popular Restaurants and Street Food

1. Traditional Flavors in Bissau City
a. Restaurante Odjos d'Agua
- **Location:** Bissau City
- **Cuisine:** Offering a blend of local and Portuguese dishes, Odjos d'Agua provides a scenic waterfront setting. Seafood enthusiasts will find an array of freshly caught delicacies.

b. Sabores da Lusofonia

- **Location:** Bissau City
- **Cuisine:** A culinary journey through Lusophone flavors, this restaurant serves dishes inspired by Portuguese-speaking cultures. The ambiance is vibrant, and the menu features a mix of seafood and meat options.

c. Restaurant Cantinho do Curioso

- **Location:** Bissau City
- **Cuisine:** Known for its cozy atmosphere and local specialties, Cantinho do Curioso offers a range of traditional dishes, including rice-based meals, grilled fish, and flavorful stews.

2. Street Food Delights

a. Bolama Street Vendors

- **Location:** Bolama Island
- **Specialties:** Explore the vibrant street food scene on Bolama Island, where local vendors offer grilled fish, kebabs, and

various snacks. Don't miss the opportunity to try cassava-based treats.

b. Bijagos Archipelago Markets

- **Location:** Various islands
- **Specialties:** Visit local markets in the Bijagos Archipelago for an authentic taste of Guinea-Bissau. Indulge in freshly caught seafood, tropical fruits, and traditional snacks prepared by skilled market vendors.

3. Culinary Experiences Beyond Bissau

a. Tchitundo-Hulo

- **Location:** Outside Bissau
- **Cuisine:** Immerse yourself in the traditional flavors of Guinea-Bissau at Tchitundo-Hulo. This cultural village not only offers guided tours but also showcases the rich culinary heritage with authentic meals prepared by locals.

b. Cacine

- **Location**: Southeastern Guinea-Bissau

- **Cuisine:** Experience the culinary diversity in the region of Cacine. Local eateries serve dishes that incorporate regional ingredients, providing a unique gastronomic adventure.

4. Dining Etiquette

- Guinea-Bissau embraces a relaxed dining culture. It is customary to greet others before starting a meal.
- Tipping is appreciated but not mandatory. If service charge is not included, a 5-10% tip is customary in restaurants.
- Engage with locals to learn about traditional dining practices, as sharing a meal often involves communal dishes.

5. Food Safety Tips

- While street food can be enticing, prioritize vendors with good hygiene practices and high customer turnover to ensure the freshness of the food.

- Drink bottled or purified water and avoid consuming raw or undercooked seafood to prevent foodborne illnesses.

Exploring the culinary scene in Guinea-Bissau provides an opportunity to savor the diverse flavors deeply rooted in its cultural heritage. From bustling markets to cozy restaurants, the country offers a delightful gastronomic experience for every traveler.

SHOPPING AND SOUVENIRS

11.1 Markets and Shopping Districts in Guinea-Bissau

Guinea-Bissau offers a vibrant and culturally rich shopping experience, with bustling markets and unique shopping districts where travelers can explore local crafts, traditional goods, and immerse themselves in the lively atmosphere. Here's a detailed overview of the markets and shopping districts in Guinea-Bissau:

Bandim Market (Mercado Bandim):
- Located in the heart of Bissau, Bandim Market is the largest and most popular market in the country.
- A colorful array of stalls selling fresh produce, spices, textiles, and handmade crafts.

- The market is an excellent place to experience the local culture, interact with vendors, and sample traditional snacks.

Bissau City Center:
- The city center is dotted with a mix of modern shops and traditional markets, offering a diverse shopping experience.
- Trendy boutiques, souvenir shops, and local artisans showcase a blend of contemporary and traditional Guinean craftsmanship.

Bolama Island Markets:
- Bolama, one of the Bijagos Islands, hosts vibrant markets where visitors can find unique handmade goods and traditional artifacts.
- Local artisans often display intricately woven baskets, wood carvings, and vibrant textiles, providing a glimpse into the region's rich cultural heritage.

Canchungo Market:

- Located in the northern part of the country, Canchungo Market is known for its agricultural products, including fresh fruits, vegetables, and locally produced goods.
- The market offers an authentic experience, with sellers dressed in traditional attire and a variety of products reflecting the local lifestyle.

Buba Market:

- Situated in the southern part of Guinea-Bissau, Buba Market is a lively hub for traders from neighboring regions.
- Visitors can explore a diverse range of products, from handmade crafts to spices and traditional medicinal herbs.

Rua 24 de Setembro:

- In the capital city, Bissau, Rua 24 de Setembro is a bustling street known for its shops and small businesses.

- Here, travelers can find a mix of modern and traditional items, including clothing, accessories, and souvenirs.

Crafts Market in Quinhamel:
- Quinhamel, known for its beautiful beaches, is also home to a crafts market.
- Local artisans showcase their skills in pottery, beadwork, and traditional mask-making, providing an opportunity to purchase unique handmade souvenirs.

Shopping Tips:
- Bargaining is a common practice in Guinea-Bissau markets, and visitors should feel free to negotiate prices.
- Cash is the preferred payment method, so it's advisable to carry local currency (West African CFA franc) when visiting markets.
- Respect local customs and ask for permission before taking photographs,

especially in markets where vendors may have religious or cultural sensitivities.

Exploring Guinea-Bissau's markets and shopping districts not only provides an opportunity for souvenir hunting but also offers a chance to engage with the local community and gain insight into the country's diverse cultural tapestry.

11.2 Unique Handicrafts and Artisanal Products

Guinea-Bissau is a treasure trove of vibrant handicrafts and artisanal products, reflecting the rich cultural tapestry of the nation. In this chapter, we delve into the unique world of local craftsmanship, highlighting the exquisite items that make for meaningful souvenirs and memorable gifts.

1. Bijagós Basketry and Weaving:
Discover the artistry of the Bijagós people through their intricate basketry and weaving techniques.

These baskets, often made from locally sourced materials, showcase both practicality and aesthetic appeal. Visitors can find an array of designs, from everyday baskets to ceremonial masterpieces.

2. Batik Fabrics:

Guinea-Bissau is renowned for its vibrant batik fabrics, reflecting the creativity and cultural heritage of the local artisans. These fabrics feature traditional patterns and symbols, with each piece telling a unique story. Visitors can purchase batik textiles in various forms, including clothing, scarves, and wall hangings.

3. Woodcarvings and Sculptures:

Local artisans skillfully carve wood into intricate sculptures, masks, and figurines, often depicting scenes from traditional rituals or symbolizing cultural beliefs. These handcrafted items make for captivating and meaningful mementos, showcasing the talent and craftsmanship of Guinea-Bissau's artists.

4. Bamboo and Raffia Products:

Embrace the eco-friendly creations made from bamboo and raffia, such as hats, bags, and decorative items. These sustainable products highlight the importance of traditional materials in contemporary design, blending functionality with a touch of authenticity.

5. Pottery and Ceramics:

Explore the world of traditional pottery and ceramics, where skilled artisans mold clay into beautifully crafted vessels, plates, and sculptures. The designs often incorporate local symbols and patterns, making each piece a unique representation of Guinea-Bissau's cultural heritage.

6. Bijagós Jewelry:

Adorn yourself with exquisite jewelry inspired by the Bijagós archipelago. Local artisans create stunning pieces using natural materials like shells, seeds, and beads. These unique accessories are not only fashionable but also carry cultural significance, making them cherished keepsakes.

7. Palm Leaf Products:

Witness the art of transforming palm leaves into practical items such as hats, mats, and baskets. The intricate weaving techniques employed by local artisans result in durable and aesthetically pleasing products, providing visitors with a glimpse into the traditional skills passed down through generations.

8. Traditional Musical Instruments:

Immerse yourself in the rhythm of Guinea-Bissau with traditional musical instruments crafted by skilled artisans. Djembes, balafons, and other percussion instruments are not only beautiful to look at but also offer a unique way to bring the country's musical heritage home.

Whether you are seeking a piece of traditional art or a functional souvenir, Guinea-Bissau's handicrafts and artisanal products offer a diverse array of choices. Purchasing these items not only supports local artisans but also allows you to take home a tangible piece of the country's vibrant culture.

11.3 Bargaining Tips

Guinea-Bissau is a place where the art of bargaining is not just a transactional skill but an integral part of the local culture. Engaging in friendly haggling can enhance your shopping experience and help you get the best value for your money. Here are some insightful tips on bargaining in Guinea-Bissau.

Establish a Friendly Rapport:
Before diving into negotiations, initiate a friendly conversation with the seller. Greetings and casual inquiries about the day are customary and lay the foundation for a positive interaction.

Understand Local Prices:
Take time to observe prices in local markets before making any purchases. Understanding the general

price range for various items will empower you to negotiate more effectively.

Start with a Smile:

Approach bargaining with a smile. A friendly demeanor can go a long way in creating a positive atmosphere for negotiations. Keep the tone light-hearted and amicable.

Practice Patience:

Bargaining in Guinea-Bissau is a gradual process. Be patient and avoid showing impatience or frustration. Taking your time demonstrates that you are genuinely interested in the item and willing to engage in a fair negotiation.

Polite Persistence:

Politely expressing your desired price and persistently sticking to it can be effective. However, be respectful in your approach, ensuring the negotiation remains a friendly exchange rather than a confrontational encounter.

Bundle Purchases:

Consider bundling multiple items from the same seller. This tactic often allows for more flexibility in pricing, as sellers may be more willing to offer discounts for bulk purchases.

Know When to Walk Away:

One of the most powerful bargaining tools is the willingness to walk away. If the seller is not meeting your desired price, politely thank them and indicate that you might explore other options. In many cases, this prompts the seller to reconsider their initial offer.

Stay Informed:

Have a general idea of the actual value of the item you're interested in. This knowledge can be useful in negotiations and prevent you from overpaying.

Use Local Phrases:

If you've picked up some basic Portuguese phrases, incorporating them into your negotiation can be a delightful touch. It shows respect for the local language and culture, and sellers may appreciate your effort.

Respect the Culture:
Bargaining in Guinea-Bissau is a cultural exchange. Be respectful, maintain a sense of humor, and avoid overly aggressive tactics. Creating a positive interaction benefits both you and the seller.

Remember, bargaining is not just about getting the lowest price; it's about building connections and enjoying the cultural experience. Embrace the process with a positive attitude, and you'll likely come away with not only great deals but also memorable encounters with the locals.

PRACTICAL TRAVEL TIP

12.1 Electricity and Plug Standards

Understanding the electricity and plug standards in Guinea-Bissau is crucial for travelers to ensure a seamless experience and the proper functioning of their electronic devices. Here is detailed information on this aspect for your Guinea-Bissau travel guide:

Voltage and Frequency:
Guinea-Bissau operates on a standard voltage of 220-240V with a frequency of 50Hz. Travelers should be aware of this when using electrical appliances and devices.

Plug Types:
The standard plug types used in Guinea-Bissau are Type C and Type F. Type C has two round pins, while Type F has two round pins with the addition

of grounding. It's advisable for travelers to carry the necessary plug adapters to match these standards.

Adapter and Converter Requirements:
Visitors from countries using different plug types (e.g., Type A or Type B) will need a suitable adapter to connect their devices to the local outlets. Additionally, if their devices are not compatible with the local voltage, a voltage converter may be necessary.

Availability of Power Outlets:
Power outlets in Guinea-Bissau are generally equipped to handle multiple plug types, making it convenient for travelers with different adapter needs. However, it's still advisable to carry a universal adapter for versatility.

Charging Stations and Availability:
In urban areas and major towns, access to charging stations and outlets for electronic devices is relatively common. However, in more remote or

rural areas, availability may be limited, so it's wise to plan ahead and carry portable chargers when necessary.

Hotels and Accommodations:

Most hotels and accommodations in Guinea-Bissau provide power outlets compatible with common plug types. It's recommended to confirm the electrical specifications with the accommodation before arrival and carry any necessary adapters.

Power Cuts and Voltage Fluctuations:

While Guinea-Bissau has a generally reliable power supply in urban areas, occasional power cuts and voltage fluctuations may occur. Travelers should be prepared for these situations by using surge protectors for sensitive electronic equipment.

Local Advice and Assistance:

If travelers have specific concerns or questions about electricity and plug standards during their stay, seeking advice from hotel staff, local residents, or travel guides can be helpful in ensuring a trouble-free experience.

By being aware of Guinea-Bissau's electricity and plug standards, travelers can plan accordingly and enjoy a hassle-free stay, ensuring that their electronic devices remain functional throughout their exploration of this vibrant West African destination.

12.2 Internet and Communication in Guinea-Bissau

Guinea-Bissau, with its unique blend of cultural richness and natural beauty, offers visitors an immersive experience. As you embark on your journey, staying connected and communicating effectively becomes crucial. This chapter provides detailed information on internet services, communication options, and tips for staying connected during your travels in Guinea-Bissau.

1. Internet Services:

- **Overview:** Guinea-Bissau has been making strides in improving its internet infrastructure, especially in urban areas like Bissau. However, it's essential to be prepared for varying levels of connectivity, particularly in more remote regions.

- **Internet Providers:** The major internet service providers include Guinetel and MTN Guinea-Bissau. Guinetel is a state-owned company, while MTN is a multinational telecommunications group. Both offer SIM cards and data plans.

2. Mobile Connectivity:

- **SIM Cards:** Visitors can easily purchase local SIM cards from providers like MTN Guinea-Bissau and use them in unlocked GSM phones. This provides access to data plans for internet use and local calls.

- **Coverage:** While major cities and towns generally have good mobile network coverage, rural areas may experience limited connectivity. It's advisable to check coverage maps and inquire locally about the best network for your specific destinations.

3. Internet Cafés and Hotspots:

- **Urban Areas:** Bissau, the capital city, hosts internet cafés and Wi-Fi hotspots in various establishments, such as hotels, restaurants, and coffee shops. These are convenient for travelers seeking a place to connect their devices.

- **Rural Areas:** In more remote areas, internet access may be limited, and internet cafés might be scarce. Plan accordingly and be prepared to rely on mobile data or Wi-Fi from accommodations.

4. Cybersecurity Considerations:

- **Public Wi-Fi:** Exercise caution when using public Wi-Fi, as cybersecurity standards may vary. Avoid accessing sensitive information or conducting financial transactions on unsecured networks.

- **Data Security:** Use virtual private networks (VPNs) for an added layer of security when accessing the internet, especially if you need to connect to public networks.

5. Communication Tips:

- **Language:** Portuguese is the official language of Guinea-Bissau. While English is not widely spoken, you can learn basic Portuguese phrases or use translation apps to facilitate communication.

- **Local Etiquette:** The people of Guinea-Bissau are generally friendly and welcoming. Politeness and respect go a long way in fostering positive interactions.

6. Emergency Numbers:

- **Police:** 119
- **Medical Emergency:** 112
- **Fire Service:** 118

While internet and communication infrastructure in Guinea-Bissau may not be as advanced as in some Western countries, the increasing efforts to improve connectivity are noticeable. Embrace the opportunity to disconnect at times and fully immerse yourself in the country's rich cultural and natural offerings.

Remember, flexibility and a sense of adventure are essential components of an enriching travel experience in Guinea-Bissau. Stay connected, but don't forget to savor the moments of being off the grid.

RESPONSIBLE TOURISM

13.1 Environmental Conservation Efforts

Guinea-Bissau, with its rich biodiversity and unique ecosystems, is actively engaged in various environmental conservation efforts aimed at preserving its natural heritage. Travelers who are environmentally conscious can participate in and support these initiatives to contribute to the sustainability of the country's ecosystems. Here's an overview of some key environmental conservation efforts in Guinea-Bissau:

Bijagos National Marine Park:

- The Bijagos Archipelago, a UNESCO Biosphere Reserve, is home to the Bijagos National Marine Park, encompassing a network of islands with diverse marine life.

- Conservation programs focus on protecting endangered species such as sea turtles and manatees through research, monitoring, and community involvement.

- Visitors can contribute by adhering to responsible tourism practices, including respecting wildlife habitats and following designated paths.

Community-Led Conservation Projects:

- Several local communities actively participate in conservation initiatives, aiming to balance the needs of the environment with sustainable livelihoods.

- Projects often involve community-based ecotourism, where travelers can engage with local communities, learning about their efforts to protect natural resources while contributing to their economic well-being.

Mangrove Restoration Initiatives:

- Mangroves play a crucial role in coastal ecosystems, providing habitat for diverse marine life and acting as a buffer against erosion and storm surges.

- Conservation organizations collaborate with local communities to restore and protect mangrove areas, promoting sustainable resource management practices.

Orango Island Wildlife Sanctuary:

- Orango Island is home to a wildlife sanctuary known for its diverse flora and fauna, including saltwater hippos and numerous bird species.
- Conservation efforts include habitat restoration, anti-poaching measures, and educational programs to raise awareness about the importance of preserving this unique environment.

Environmental Education Programs:

- NGOs and local organizations run environmental education programs to raise awareness among local communities and visitors about the importance of conservation.

- Travelers can engage in these programs to learn about the delicate balance between human activities and the preservation of Guinea-Bissau's natural resources.

Waste Management Initiatives:

- To combat plastic pollution and promote sustainable waste management practices, communities and conservation organizations organize clean-up campaigns and recycling initiatives.
- Travelers are encouraged to minimize their environmental footprint by disposing of waste responsibly and supporting businesses that prioritize eco-friendly practices.

Biosphere Reserve Protection:

- Guinea-Bissau has designated certain areas as Biosphere Reserves to promote sustainable development and biodiversity conservation.

- Travelers can contribute by respecting designated conservation zones, adhering to responsible tourism guidelines, and supporting businesses committed to environmental sustainability.

By actively participating in and supporting these environmental conservation efforts, travelers can contribute to the long-term preservation of Guinea-Bissau's natural beauty and cultural heritage, ensuring that future generations can continue to appreciate and enjoy this unique destination.

13.2 Cultural Respect and Responsible Behavior

Guinea-Bissau, with its rich cultural tapestry and diverse traditions, welcomes visitors with open arms. To ensure a positive and respectful travel experience, it's crucial for tourists to understand and adhere to cultural norms and responsible behavior. Here's a detailed guide on how to show cultural respect and practice responsible tourism in Guinea-Bissau:

Greet Locals with Respect:

The traditional greeting in Guinea-Bissau is warm and involves a handshake accompanied by a few pleasantries. Take the time to greet locals respectfully, and be open to engaging in friendly conversations.

Dress Modestly:

While the climate can be hot, particularly in coastal areas, it's advisable to dress modestly, especially when visiting religious sites and rural communities. Avoid overly revealing clothing to show respect for local customs.

Photography Etiquette:

Always seek permission before taking photographs, especially of people. Some individuals may have cultural or personal reasons for not wanting their pictures taken, and it's essential to respect their wishes.

Respect Religious Practices:

Guinea-Bissau is home to various religious beliefs, including Islam, Christianity, and indigenous animist practices. Be mindful of religious sites and ceremonies, and dress modestly when entering places of worship.

Participate Respectfully in Traditions:

If you have the opportunity to participate in local traditions or ceremonies, do so with genuine interest and respect. Ask questions to better understand the significance of the rituals and celebrations.

Support Local Businesses:

Opt to support local businesses, markets, and artisans. This helps contribute to the local economy and ensures that the benefits of tourism reach the communities directly.

Learn Basic Local Phrases:

Although Portuguese is the official language, learning a few basic phrases in Creole or other local languages can go a long way in building rapport with the locals. They will appreciate your effort to communicate in their language.

Be Mindful of Environmental Impact:

Guinea-Bissau boasts pristine natural landscapes. Practice responsible tourism by avoiding littering, following designated trails, and supporting eco-friendly initiatives. Respect the delicate balance of the environment and wildlife.

Ask Permission Before Entering Homes:

If invited into a local's home, remember to ask for permission before entering. It's a customary gesture that reflects respect for the residents and their personal space.

Be Open to Cultural Differences:

Guinea-Bissau is culturally diverse, and customs can vary between regions and ethnic groups. Approach cultural differences with an open mind and a willingness to learn, fostering a deeper appreciation for the local way of life.

Practice Responsible Wildlife Viewing:
If engaging in wildlife activities, such as birdwatching or exploring nature reserves, follow ethical guidelines to minimize disturbance to the animals and their habitats. Respect local conservation efforts and regulations.

By embracing cultural respect and responsible behavior, travelers can forge meaningful connections with the people of Guinea-Bissau and contribute to the preservation of its rich cultural heritage and natural beauty.

APPENDIX

14.1 Useful Phrases in Portuguese

Portuguese is the official language of Guinea-Bissau, and while many locals may speak some basic English or French, knowing a few Portuguese phrases can greatly enhance your travel experience and interactions with the friendly locals. Here are some useful phrases to help you navigate through Guinea-Bissau:

Basic Greetings:
- **Hello** - Olá
- **Good morning** - Bom dia
- **Good afternoon** - Boa tarde
- **Good evening** - Boa noite
- **Goodbye** - Adeus

Common Courtesies:
- **Please** - Por favor

- **Thank you** - Obrigado (if you're male) / Obrigada (if you're female)
- **You're welcome** - De nada
- **Excuse me / I'm sorry** - Desculpe

Getting Around:
- **Where is...?** - Onde fica...?
- **How much is this?** - Quanto custa?
- **I need a taxi** - Preciso de um táxi
- **Where is the bus station?** - Onde é a estação de autocarros?

Eating and Drinking:
- **I would like to order...** - Eu gostaria de pedir...
- **Water** - Água
- **Menu** - Cardápio
- **Delicious!** - Delicioso!

Navigating Accommodations:
- **Room** - Quarto
- **Reservation** - Reserva

- **Check-in** / **Check-out** - Check-in / Check-out

Emergency Phrases:
- **Help!** - Socorro!
- - Preciso de um médico
- **Where is the nearest hospital?** - Onde fica o hospital mais próximo?

Shopping:
- **How much does it cost?** - Quanto custa?
- **I'll take it** - Eu vou levar

Numbers:
- **1-10** - Um, dois, três, quatro, cinco, seis, sete, oito, nove, dez

Days and Time:
- **Today** / **Tomorrow** / **Yesterday** - Hoje / Amanhã / Ontem
- **Monday to Sunday** - Segunda-feira a Domingo

- **Morning / Afternoon / Evening** - Manhã / Tarde / Noite

Socializing:
- **What's your name?** - Qual é o seu nome?
- **My name is**... - Meu nome é…
- **Cheers!** - Saúde!

Learning these basic Portuguese phrases will not only facilitate smoother communication but also demonstrate your respect for the local culture. The people of Guinea-Bissau are welcoming, and your effort to speak their language will be appreciated. Enjoy your travels in this vibrant and diverse country!

14.2 Maps and Diagrams

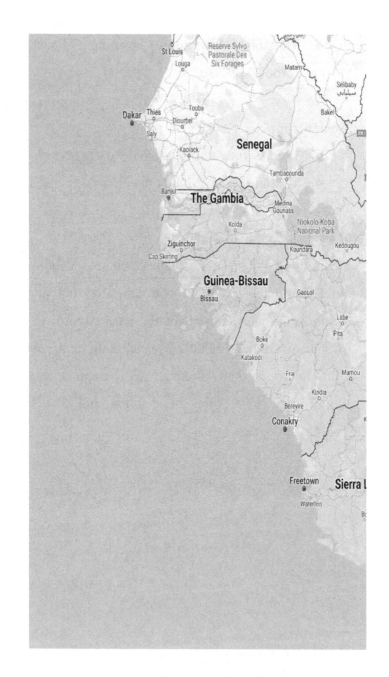

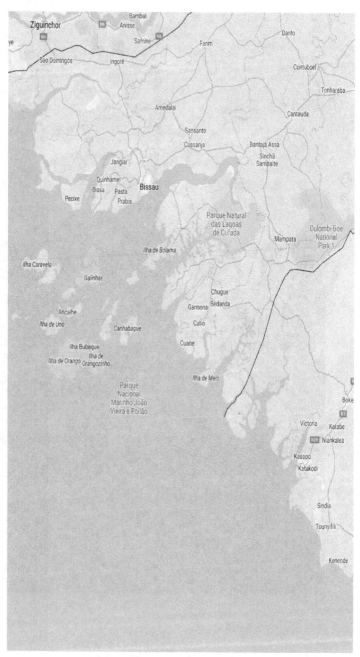

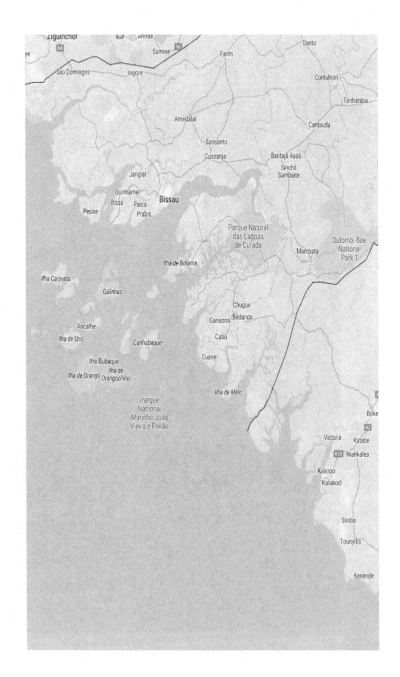